Handy California Genealogy Handbook

I0450532

Gary L. Morris

©2015 Gary L. Morris

ISBN-13: 978-1507745007

ISBN-10: 1507745001

Table of Contents

Notes

Genealogical Research in California

California is especially interesting to genealogists because of its ethnic and cultural diversity. Although researching California records presents a unique set of challenges, it also has its own unique rewards. There are many historical and genealogical records available for the state, and we know just where to find them. To get you started in tracing your ancestry, we'll introduce you to those records, and help you to understand:

        1.   What they are
        2.   Where to find them
        3.   How to use them

These records can be found both online and off, so we'll introduce you to online websites, indexes and databases, as well as brick-and-mortar repositories and other institutions that will help with your research in California. So that you will have a more comprehensive understanding of these records, we have provided a brief history of the "The Golden State" to illustrate what type of records may have been generated during specific time periods. That information will assist you in pinpointing times and locations on which to focus the search for your California ancestors.

A Brief History of California

In 1765 a representative of the King of Spain arrived in California, then called New Spain, to establish Spanish control in the region. Missions and forts to protect the Spanish settlers were established, and the Native American population were welcomed into the fold. The establishments of the forts and missions led to the growth of towns to supply them, known as pueblos. These pueblos eventually became cities that today we know as San Francisco, Los Angeles, and Monterey.

In 1810 the inhabitants of this "New Spain" began a war to fight for their independence from Spain. They achieved victory in 1821, and established their own government before the Mexican government seized control of the region. The Mexican government proceeded to take land from the original settlers and distribute it to Mexican settlers and the Native Americans who had settled in to the missions. The land that was taken from the missions was given as land grants, thus generating valuable genealogical documentation.

Before long Russia developed an interest in California and Russian hunters built a settlement in the northern area of the state called Fort Ross. By 1841 the scores of sea lions, seals, and otters that the hunters had originally come for was severely depleted, and the Russians sold Fort Ross and deserted the area. Beaver trappers also began moving into the area at this time, and established a base in the San Joaquin Valley. The most important aspect of the settlement of trappers was that it showed other settlers on the North American continent that there was a land route into California.

As this knowledge reached mainstream America, the desire of the United States to expand westward was flamed. This led to the development of the Manifest Destiny, which was basically a declaration of the United States to annex New Mexico, Texas, and California.

A group of rebellious American settlers imprisoned a Mexican general in 1846 and declared California a "free state." They raise a flag emblazoned with a grizzly bear and a star with the words "California Republic" in Sonoma, a revolt which led to war between the United States and Mexico beginning on May 13, 1846. By 1848 the war was over, and Mexico agreed to cede California to the United States. Gold was discovered in the Sierra Nevada Mountains in the same year, leading to what would become the largest mass migration in the world's history; a migration we today know as the "California Gold Rush."

In just four short years between 1848 and 1852, the population of California grew from a meager 14,000 inhabitants to a population of nearly 250,000. Those seeking gold came from all over the world, including Australia, China, Europe, and America itself. This influx of people and the discovery of gold led to an economic boom in California, which in turn led to the growth of other industries and commerce. California was granted statehood in 1850, and when the Union Pacific Railroad linked California with Utah in 1869, the state began to grow into the multicultural, prosperous state we know today.

Important Genealogical Dates in California History

1768 – First Spanish governor appointed

1812 – Fort Ross established by Russians

1821 – Becomes province of Mexico

1837 – Mexican laws adopted

1846 – US forces occupy San Diego and San Francisco

1848 – Acquired from Mexico in Treaty of Guadalupe-Hildago, gold discovered.

1850 – Statehood

1906 – San Francisco Earthquake.

Famous Battles Fought in California

Many battles were fought in California during the Mexican American War, and there are some service records from this time that were generated. The battle accounts themselves can be very effective in uncovering the military records of your ancestor. They can tell you what regiments fought in which battles, and often include the names and ranks of many officers and enlisted men. Following are some of the most famous battles fought in California and links to useful information about them.

Battle of Palo Alto, 1846: http://www.history.com/topics/battle-of-palo-alto

Battle of Resaca de la Palma, 1846: http://www.history.army.mil/brochures/Resaca%20de%20la%20Palma/Palo%20Alto.htm

Battle of Monterey, 1846: http://www.militarymuseum.org/Monterey1.html

Battle of Buena Vista, 1847: http://www.britannica.com/EBchecked/topic/83513/Battle-of-Buena-Vista

Common California Genealogical Issues and Resources to Overcome Them

Boundary Changes: Boundary changes are a common obstacle when researching California ancestors. You could be searching for an ancestor's record in one county when in fact it is stored in a different one due to historical county boundary changes. The **Atlas of Historical County Boundaries** can help you to overcome that problem. It provides a chronological listing of every boundary change that has occurred in the history of California.

Atlas of Historical County Boundaries:
http://publications.newberry.org/ahcbp/documents/CA_Consolidated _Chronology.htm#Consolidated_Chronology

Name Changes: Surname changes, variations, and misspellings can complicate genealogical research. It is important to check all spelling variations. Soundex, a program that indexes names by sound, is a useful first step, but you can't rely on it completely as some name variations result in different Soundex codes. The surnames could be different, but the first name may be different too. You can also find records filed under initials, middle names, and nicknames as well, so you will need to **get creative with surname variations** and spellings in order to cover all the possibilities. For help with surname variations read our instructional article on **How to Use Soundex**.

get creative with surname variations:
http://obituarieshelp.org/blog/?p=634

How to Use Soundex link to: http://obituarieshelp.org/blog/?p=505

California Genealogical Organizations and Archives

Genealogical resources include not only records, but the organizations that house them, or can direct you to them. These institutions include: *Archives, Libraries, Genealogical Societies, Family History Centers, Universities, Churches, and Museums.*

Following are links to their websites, their physical addresses, and a summary of the records you can find there.

California Archives

California State Archives – census schedules, property records, county records, court records, military records, school records, and business records

California State Archives
1020 O Street
Sacramento, CA 95814

Tel: (Reference Desk) - 916 653–2246
Fax: 916 653–7363
Email: via online contact form

California State Archives:
http://www.sos.ca.gov/archives/collections/family-history-resources.htm

California State Library – census records, voter registrations, city and county directories, historical newspapers, death index

California State Library
P. O. Box 942837
Sacramento, CA 94237-0001
Tel: 916-654-0261
Fax: 916-654-0241
E-Mail: cslsirc@library.ca.gov

California State Library:
http://www.library.ca.gov/calhist/genealogy.html

The Bancroft Library – rare books, historical photos, land maps, manuscripts, ethnic collections

The Bancroft Library
University of California
Berkeley, CA 94720-6000
Tel: (510) 642-6481 (Reference Desk)
Fax: 510 642-7589

The Bancroft Library: http://bancroft.berkeley.edu/collections/

Carlsbad City Library – printed books, journals, city directories, county histories, county atlases, state census reports

Carlsbad City Library
1250 Carlsbad Village Drive
Carlsbad, CA 92008
Tel: 760-434-2931

Carlsbad City Library:
http://www.carlsbadca.gov/services/departments/library/research/Pages/genealogy.aspx

California Genealogical and Historical Societies

Genealogical and historical societies have access to extensive catalogues of genealogical data. They are also able to offer expert guidance for genealogical researchers. Many members are professional genealogists who are most willing to share their expertise in finding ancestors.

California Historical Society (North Baker Research Library) – books, periodicals, historical newspapers, manuscripts, historical photograph collection, narratives, diaries, journals

The California Historical Society
678 Mission Street
San Francisco, California 94105
Telephone: 415-357-1848
Fax: 415-357-1850

California Historical Society:
http://www.californiahistoricalsociety.org/research/

Society of California Pioneers – historical books, manuscripts, Gold Rush materials, maps, historical photographs

300 Fourth Street
San Francisco, CA 94107-1272
Tel: 415-957-1849
Fax: 415-957-9858
EMail: info@californiapioneers.org

Society of California Pioneers: http://www.californiapioneers.org/

California Genealogical Society and Library – surnames, religious records, burial permits, cemetery records, school records, genealogies

2201 Broadway, Suite LL2
Oakland, CA 94612-3031
Tel: 510-663-1358
Fax: 510-663-1596

California Genealogical Society and Library:
http://www.scgsgenealogy.com/free/search-free-data.html

Southern California Genealogical Society Library

417 Irving Drive
Burbank, CA. 91504
Tel: 818 843-7247
Fax: 818-843-7262

Southern California Genealogical Society Library:
http://www.scgsgenealogy.com/

California Family History Centers

The Family History Centers run by the LDS Church offer free access to billions of genealogical records for free to the general public. They also provide classes on genealogy and one-on-one assistance to inexperienced family historians. Here you will find a **Complete Listing of California Family History Centers**.

Complete Listing of California Family History Centers:
https://familysearch.org/locations/centerlocator

California Mailing Lists

Mailing lists are internet based facilities that use email to distribute a single message to all who subscribe to it. When information on a particular surname, new records, or any other important genealogy information related to the mailing list topic becomes available, the subscribers are alerted to it. Joining a mailing list is an excellent way to stay up to date on California genealogy research topics. Rootsweb have an extensive listing of **California Mailing Lists** on a variety of topics.

California Mailing Lists:
http://lists.rootsweb.ancestry.com/index/usa/CA/misc.html

California Message Boards

A message board is another internet based facility where people can post questions about a specific genealogy topic and have it answered by other genealogists. If you have questions about a surname, record type, or research topic, you can post your question and other researchers and genealogists will help you with the answer. Be sure to check back regularly, as the answers are not emailed to you. The California message boards at **Rootsweb** are completely free to use.

Rootsweb:
http://boards.rootsweb.com/localities.northam.usa.states/mb.ashx

California Newspapers and Periodicals

Many genealogy periodicals and historical newspapers contain reprinted copies of family genealogies, transcripts of family Bible records, information about local records and archives, census indexes, church records, queries, land records, obituaries, court records, cemetery records, and wills. The following sites have historical California newspapers and periodicals that you can search online or on-site.

NewspaperArchive.com – largest online database of historical newspapers in the world.

NewspaperArchive.com: http://newspaperarchive.com/

USC Libraries – historical newspaper database

USC Libraries:
http://libguides.usc.edu/content.php?pid=39960&sid=2993338

Newspaper and Periodical Indexes for California – newspapers and periodicals from 1846

Newspaper and Periodical Indexes for California:
http://bancroft.berkeley.edu/reference/newsindexes.html

Historical California Maps and Gazetteers

Maps are an integral part of genealogical research. They help us to
locate landmarks, towns, cities, parishes, states, provinces,
waterways and roads and streets. They also help us to determine
when and where boundary changes might have taken place, and give
us a visualization of the area we're researching in. For locating place
names, a gazetteer is the best possible resource for any genealogist.
Gazetteers are also sometimes called "place name dictionaries", and
can help you to locate the area in which you need to conduct
research. Below are links to the maps and gazetteers for research in
California.

Peabody GNIS Service – California:
http://peabody.research.yale.edu/cgi-
bin/Query.GNIS?ST=California&SU=1

Color Landform Atlas – California:
http://fermi.jhuapl.edu/states/ca_0.html

1985 U.S. Atlas: http://www.livgenmi.com/1895/CA/

California Hometown Locator:
http://california.hometownlocator.com/

California City Directories

City directories are similar to telephone directories in that they list the residents of a particular area. The difference though is what is important to genealogists, and that is they pre-date telephone directories. You can find an ancestor's information such as their street address, place of employment, occupation, or the name of their spouse. A one-stop-shop for finding city directories in California is the **California Online Historical Directories** which contains a listing of every available city and historical directory related to California.

California Online Historical Directories:
https://sites.google.com/site/onlinedirectorysite/Home/usa/ca

The California History Room at the **California State Library** has city and county directories in several formats: paper, microfilm, and microfiche. Their database allows you to determine if the specific city directory you need exists, and lets you know the format and location.

Special Collections
California State Library Building
900 N Street, Room 230
Sacramento, CA 95814
Tel:(916) 653-0101

California State Library: http://www.library.ca.gov/

The **Fullerton Public Library** is in the process of digitizing many historical California city directories from 1899 till late 20th century.

353 W. Commonwealth Ave.
Fullerton, CA 92832 714-738-6333
Tel: 714-738-6333

Fullerton Public Library: http://fullertonlibrary.org/city-directories/

California Genealogical Records

Birth, Death, Marriage and Divorce Records – Birth, death, and marriage records are the most basic, yet most important records attached to your ancestor. They are generally referred to as vital records as they record vital life events. The reason for their importance is that they not only place your ancestor in a specific place at a definite time, but potentially connect the individual to other relatives. Below is a list of repositories where you can find California vital records

California Centers for Disease Control and Protection – birth, death marriage and divorce records

CA Department of Public Health - Vital Records
MS: 5103
P.O. Box 997410
Sacramento, CA 95899-7410

California Centers for Disease Control and Protection:
http://www.cdc.gov/nchs/w2w/california.htm

NorCal Genealogy – US Army California births (1840-1905), 1905-1996 California Birth Index, Western States marriage index, California county marriages 1850-1952, California Marriage indexes 1949-1986, California Death indexes, 1905-2000

NorCal Genealogy:
http://www.sfgenealogy.com/norcal/caldata.htm#calvitals

California Department of Public Health – Birth, death, and marriage records listed by City and County. Listings include contact information for the registrar in each county.

California Department of Public Health:
http://www.cdph.ca.gov/certlic/birthdeathmar/Pages/CountyRecorderOffice.aspx

Census Reports

Census records are among the most important genealogical documents for placing your ancestor in a particular place at a specific time. Like BDM records, they can also lead you to other ancestors, particularly those who were living under the authority of the head of household.

California census records exist from 1790 -1940 and many images and indexes can be viewed online. Following are the best places to find California census records.

California State Archives –1852 State, 1860 and 1880 Federal census schedules

California State Archives
1020 O Street
Sacramento, CA 95814

Tel: (Reference Desk) - 916 653–2246
Fax: 916 653–7363
Email: via online contact form

California State Archives:
http://www.sos.ca.gov/archives/collections/family-history-resources.htm

U.S National Archives – Federal census records on microfilm available from 1790 to 1940.

The National Archives and Records Administration
8601 Adelphi Road
College Park, MD 20740-6001

Toll Free:1-866-272-6272
Tel:1-86-NARA-NARA
Fax: 301-837-0483

U.S National Archives: http://www.archives.gov/research/census/

California Spanish Genealogy – 1790 census transcription

California Spanish Genealogy:
http://www.sfgenealogy.com/spanish/cen1790.htm

Family Search – 1850-1940

Family Search:
https://familysearch.org/learn/wiki/en/California_Census

California Church Records

The first Catholic missions were organized in 1769, and most records start in 1770 and have been microfilmed. **The Bancroft Library** has a comprehensive of the early records.

The Bancroft Library: http://bancroft.berkeley.edu/collections/

Many of the original records generated by the missions have been gathered into central repositories. These include:

Archival Center for the Archdiocese of Los Angeles
15151 San Fernando Mission Boulevard
Mission Hills, CA 91345
Tel: (818) 365-1501
Fax: (818) 361-3276

Archival Center for the Archdiocese of Los Angeles:
http://www.la-archdiocese.org/Pages/default.aspx

Diocese of Monterey
P.O. Box 2048
Monterey, CA 93942
Tel: (831) 373-4345

Diocese of Montereyo: http://www.dioceseofmonterey.org/

Diocese of Sacramento Historical Archives
2110 Broadway
Sacramento, CA 95818
Tel: (916) 733-0299

Diocese of Sacramento Historical Archives: http://www.diocese-sacramento.org/diocese/archives.html

Archdiocese of San Francisco Archives
St. Patrick Seminary
320 Middlefield Road
Menlo Park, CA 94025
Tel: (650) 328-6502

Archdiocese of San Francisco Archives:
http://www.sfarchdiocese.org/about-us/departments-and-
offices/office-of-the-archives/?search=archives

Diocese of San Diego
3888 Paducah Drive
San Diego, CA 92117

Mailing Address
P.O. Box 85728
San Diego, CA 92186-5728
Tel: (858) 490-8200
Fax: (858) 490-8272

Diocese of San Diego: http://www.diocese-sdiego.org/

Methodist

Holt-Atherton Church Archives
University of the Pacific
3601 Pacific Avenue
Stockton, CA 95211
Tel: (209) 946-2404
Fax: (209) 946-2810

Holt-Atherton Church Archives;
http://www.pacific.edu/Library.html

Presbyterian

San Francisco Theological Seminary Library
105 Seminary Road
San Anselmo, CA 94960
Tel: (415) 451-2845

San Francisco Theological Seminary Libraryo:
http://www.sfts.edu/student/library_sfts.asp

Evangelical Lutheran Church in America

ELCA Region 2 Archives
Pacific Lutheran Theological Seminary
2770 Marin Avenue
Berkeley, CA 94708-1597
(510) 524-5264
EMail: archives@plts.edu

Evangelical Lutheran Church in America:
http://www.elca.org/who-we-are/history/elca-archives/regional-archives.aspx

California Military Records

More than 40 million Americans have participated in some time of war service since America was colonized. The chance of finding your ancestor amongst those records is exceptionally high. Military records can even reveal individuals who never actually served, such as those who registered for the two World Wars but were never called to duty.

Below are a number of links to websites and archives that contain California military records.

U.S. National Archives – WWI Draft registration cards, casualties lists, WWI and WWII service records, Korean War records, Vietnam War records, Civil War and Spanish-American War records, and casualties lists.

U.S. National Archives:
http://www.archives.gov/research/military/veterans/online.html

US Department of Veterans Affairs Nationwide Gravesite Locator – includes information on veterans and their family members buried in veterans and military cemeteries having a government grave marker.

US Department of Veterans Affairs Nationwide Gravesite Locator: http://gravelocator.cem.va.gov/

United States Index to Indian Wars Pension Files, 1892-1926 – military pension records of soldiers who fought in the Indian Wars between 1817 and 1898

United States Index to Indian Wars Pension Files, 1892-1926: https://familysearch.org/search/collection/1979427

Civil War Soldiers Service Records - Service records for both Union and Confederate soldiers indexed by soldier's name, rank, and unit.

Civil War Soldier Service Records:
http://go.fold3.com/civilwar_records/

Sons of Union Veterans of the Civil War- Grand Army of the Republic (GAR)
Posts in the State of California

Sons of Union Veterans of the Civil War:
http://suvcw.org/garposts/ca.pdf

Roster of Officers of Stevenson's Regiment – Roster of New York regiment of one thousand soldiers was sent by the US Government to California

Roster of Officers of Stevenson's Regiment:
http://www.sfgenealogy.com/sf/history/hb75yap4.htm

U.S. Casualties - Battle of Cerro Gordo, Mexico, April 18, 1847 – casualty list of American soldiers killed during the famous battle

U.S. Casualties - Battle of Cerro Gordo, Mexico, April 18, 1847:
http://www.latinamericanstudies.org/cerro-gordo/cerro-gordo-casualties.htm

California Cemetery Records

As convenient as it is to search cemetery records online, keep in mind that there are a few disadvantages over visiting a cemetery in person. They are:

- Tombstone information is not always accurately transcribed
- The arrangement of the graves in a cemetery can be crucial as family members are often buried next to each other or in the same grave. This arrangement is not always preserved in the alphabetical indexes that are found online.

With that information in mind, the following websites have databases that can be searched online for California Cemetery records.

California Tombstone Transcription Project - death and burial records

California Tombstone Transcription Project:
http://www.usgwtombstones.org/california/californ.html

African American Cemeteries Online – African American, slave, and Native American cemetery records

African American Cemeteries Online:
http://africanamericancemeteries.com/ar/

Access Genealogy – huge database of California cemetery record transcriptions

Access Genealogy:
http://www.accessgenealogy.com/cemetery/california.htm

Find a Grave – over 100 million grave records can be searched on this site. Search can be conducted by name, location, or cemetery name.

Find a Grave: http://www.findagrave.com/

Interment.net - A free online database containing approximately 4 million cemetery records from around the world.

Interment.net: http://www.interment.net/

Billion Graves – as the name implies, you can search a billion records including headstone photos, transcriptions, cemetery records, and grave locations.

Billion Graves:
http://billiongraves.com/pages/search/index.php#cemetery

California Obituaries

Obituaries can reveal a wealth about our ancestor and other relatives. You can search our **California Newspaper Obituaries Listings** from hundreds of California newspapers online for free.

California Newspaper Obituaries Listings:
http://obituarieshelp.org/california_newspaper_obituaries.html

California Wills and Probate Records

The documents found in a probate packet may include a complete inventory of a person's estate, newspaper entries, witness testimony, a copy of a will, list of debtors and creditors, names of executors or trustees, names of heirs. They can not only tell you about the ancestor you're currently researching, but lead to other ancestors. Most of these records must be accessed at a county court or clerk's office, but some can be found online as well.

The earliest California probate records were kept by the probate courts in individual counties. Since 1879 the superior court in each county has held the jurisdiction over probates, though the county clerk is normally the custodian of these records.

You can obtain copies of the original probate records by writing to the appropriate **California County Clerk**.

Many records of Nevada, Marin, Mendocino, Humboldt, Nevada, Sonoma, and Sutter counties are at the **California State Archives**. The **Family History Library** has copies of some probate records, including 33,000 wills filed in San Francisco between 1906 and 1922 on 127 microfilms.

California County Clerk:
http://www.cdph.ca.gov/certlic/birthdeathmar/pages/countyrecorderoffice.aspx

California State Archives:
http://www.sos.ca.gov/archives/collections/

Family History Library:
http://familysearch.org/learn/wiki/en/Family_History_Library

California Immigration and Naturalization Records

The naturalization process generated many types of records, including petitions, declarations of intention, and oaths of allegiance. These records can provide family historians with information such as a person's birth date and place of birth, immigration year, marital status, spouse information, occupation, witnesses' names and addresses, and more.

National Archives and Records Administration in San Bruno, California records of almost 250,000 people who attempted to immigrate through San Francisco and Honolulu during the era of the Chinese Exclusion Acts, 1882-1943.

National Archives and Records Administration in San Bruno, California: http://www.archives.gov/locations/

California, Northern U.S. District Court Naturalization Index, 1852-1989 - index to naturalization records generated in the district and circuit courts of Northern California.

California, Northern U.S. District Court Naturalization Index, 1852-1989: https://familysearch.org/search/collection/1849982

California, Southern District Court (Central) Naturalization Index, 1915-1976 - 273,000 naturalization index cards of the U.S. District Court for the Southern District of California

California, Southern District Court (Central) Naturalization Index, 1915-1976: https://familysearch.org/search/collection/1849628

California, San Diego Naturalization Index, 1868-1958 – records of individuals naturalized by the Superior Court of San Diego

California, San Diego Naturalization Index, 1868-1958: https://familysearch.org/search/collection/1840471

California, San Francisco Passenger Lists, 1893-1953: https://familysearch.org/search/collection/1916078

Native American Records

Access Genealogy – California Native American census records, tribal histories, and much more

Access Genealogy link to:
http://www.accessgenealogy.com/native/california-indian-tribes.htm

U.S. National Archives - information on American Indians who maintained their ties to Federally-recognized Tribes (1830-1970).

U.S. National Archives link to:
http://www.archives.gov/research/native-americans/

Records of the Bureau of Indian Affairs (BIA)

Records of the Bureau of Indian Affairs (BIA):
http://www.archives.gov/research/guide-fed-records/groups/075.html

American Indians Records Repository - records dating from the 1700s including trust, education and other historic Indian Affairs records

American Indian Records Repository
Meritex Enterprises
17501 West 98th Street
Lenexa, KS 66219
Phone: 913-888-0601

American Indians Records Repository:
http://www.doi.gov/ost/records_mgmt/american-indian-records-repository.cfm

Missing Matriarchs – Resources for Researching Female California Ancestors

Looking for female ancestors requires an adjustment of how we view traditional records sources. A woman's identity was often under that of her husband, and often individual records for them can be difficult to locate. The following resources are effective in locating female ancestors in California where traditional records may not reveal them.

Marriage and Divorce Records

The parish registers of the California missions hold the earliest marriage records which may be found in the archives of individual missions. The California State Archives has the Mission San Luis Obispo de Tolosa registers, 1772-1906 on microfilm (film 0913300). Other records have been filmed as follows:

1. Calaveras County recorder marriage records, 1854-1905 (film 1302999 ff.) at the Calaveras County Government Center in San Andreas.
2. Los Angeles County Clerk marriage applications 1850-1905, and marriage certificates and index, 1851-1919 (film 1033120 ff.) at the Los Angeles County Courthouse in Los Angeles.

Bibliographies

- *From Canton to California: The Epic of Chinese Immigration*, Corrine K. Hoexter (Four Winds Press, 1976)
- *Covered Wagon Women: Diaries and Letters from the Western Trails, 1852, the California Trail*, Kenneth L. Holmes, Vol. 4 (University of Nebraska Press, 1997)
- *Blacks in Gold Rush California*, Rudolph Lapp (Yale University Press, 1977)
- *California Women: A History*, Jensen Lothrop (Heinle and Heinle Publishing, 1988)

- *Spanish-Mexican Families of Early California, 1769-1850, 2 vols.,* Marie E. Northrop (Polyanthos, 1976)

Selected Resources for California Women's History

Women's Heritage Museum
870 Market St.
San Francisco, CA 94102

Women's History Reclamation Project
1436 31st St.
San Diego, CA 92102

Ella Strong Denison Library
Scripps College
1030 Colombia
Claremont, CA 91711

National Women's History Project
7738 Bell Road
Windsor, CA 95492-8518

Common California Surnames

The following surnames are among the most common in California. The list is by no means exhaustive. If your surname doesn't appear in the list it doesn't mean that you have no California connections, only that your surname may be less common.

Aitken, Arthur, Amador, Aguilar, Arnese, Ballard, Bennetts, Baldridge, Blodgett, Baldwin, Brooks, Bradley, Bratton, Buelna, Caminetti, Campi, Cottingham, Carlisle, Crocker, Courtright, Castle, Cain, Casenave, Culver, Combs, Campini, Camacho, Cassinelli, Clark, Cleveland, Cioni, Depenau, Davis, Dunlap, Dallas, Darling,De La Vega, Dominguez, Dorrell, Dolan, Dabb, Dempsey, Downey, Ekel, Epling, Enrico, Feenan, Fleehart, Francisco, Fox, Galindo, Garcia, Giovanni, Gonzalez, Gordon, Gooding, Gibson, Howard, Harris, Hernandez, Higuera, Jackson, Jordan, Jones, Kinney, Kelly, Leon, Lopez, Lozano, Mandana, Murphy, Morrison, McGriff, Mugford, Martinez, Martell, Moglich, McNeil, Manahan, Machado, Morales, Moreno, Najera, Noce, Nichols, Nicolaus, Olivares, Ortega, Oneto, Oats, Orlandi, Potter, Plasse, Purington, Pacheco, Peralta, Perez, Ramos, Rodriguez, Rojos, Rogers, Ruffner, Rock, Rice, Ringer, Sallee, Strong, Simmons, Sapunar, Sexton, Sanchez, Soto, Torres, Thompson, Torre, Tanner, Valencia, Valenzuela, Villa, Yorba

About the Author

Gary L. Morris worked from 2009 to 2014 as a professional researcher for a major player in the genealogy field. After tracing his family lineage back to 1683, he found that genealogy could be an expensive undertaking. As such, has decided to publish these helpful guides to share the valuable free information he has discovered during his career to help others trace their family lineages as inexpensively as possible. An avid genealogist himself, he hopes you will find this guide factual, thorough, helpful, and most of all, effective in helping you to find your family members.

Notes

Notes